MAKE MINE

DIVINE

I0164436

MESSAGES
from the LIGHT
to Illuminate
Your Day

HEMAT MALAK

Make Mine Divine

Messages from the Light
to Illuminate Your Day

ISBN: 978-0-9874508-3-8

Published in Australia

For the Divine

in each of us

What others are saying about
MAKE MINE DIVINE

"This book by Hemat Malak is truly inspired from the Light. Be inspired by these angel Light messages, and transform to a higher vibration—this is a priceless gift for your soul."

—*Michele Blood, best-selling author and mystical teacher*

"As I was reading through these short messages, my attention was drawn inward to my heart. When I read "Discomfort," I felt a little laugh inside of me. It was like the words were drawing up the joy inside of me. That was a wonderful feeling. It was like the words were speaking to my inner being."

—*William Scannell, Ireland*

"These are truly messages from the Light, and they are filled with Love, Light and TRUTH. I simply go into the silence and open this book; each time without fail, the page opens to the perfect message for me. Not only do they illuminate your day, but your whole life, your heart and your very soul. I am so thankful to

Hemat for gifting the world with these beautiful, Divine messages."

—*Zobeeda Madsen, author of the book series, "Autism, the Language of Love"*

"It's simply BEAUTIFUL!"
- *Ciprian Vaida, France*

"One of the finest books to brighten anybody's day, motivating and inspiring to go ahead, live each day with heart-centered alignment and feel your magnificence beyond the illusions, making every day GRAND!"
- *Jasvinder K Husson, USA*

"The words in this book bring so much clarity if you read them as words from the Divine and not just mere words. This book has done wonders for my soul. Thank you, Hemat!"
- *Julia Hines, USA*

"I **love** Hemat's book! Even as I glance through it, I feel immense peace. The messages speak directly to my heart and feel so true. Thank you, Hemat, for making these messages available."
- *Ruth Donald, Australia*

"I am so grateful to read the words...every word...touches my heart, motivates me to brighten my day. Thank you very much."
- *Paramesvary Perumal, Malaysia*

Foreword

I am happy to write the foreword to this beautiful second book by Hemat Malak. I have experienced my own awakening and see and feel the Truth in these words from the Light.

I personally know Hemat, and her inspiration is real and pure. As you read these messages that I call *Light poems*, you can transform to a higher vibration, and this is a priceless gift for your soul.

Poetry can speak to the soul, and these messages from on High tap into the Divine Dimension and lift you there.

A useful exercise of soul would be to select any page at random and find in the words their Divine Dimension; this will be a message you will KNOW is just for you.

Dive deeply into this book, drink and be refreshed.

This book can provide a rich and expansive opening that may lead one to a journey of self-discovery. These messages resonate across time and space at the core of all human spirits. This will be a joy own.

As you read the words and something touches you deeply, simply stop for a moment, for that is the Light awakening your spirit. Read, contemplate and *transform*.

Make Mine Divine is a collection of spiritual wisdom that can lift you to the richness of your soul.

—Michele Blood

Michele Blood is a best-selling author of over 90 books, audio programs and DVDs on self-discovery. Her most recent book was co-authored with Bob Proctor.

www.Musivation.com

www.MysticalSuccessClub.com

Contents

Acknowledgments

Support is a blessing, and I have been blessed again with wonderful support in the creation of this book.

To my two precious children, Bianca and Leo, thank you for bringing joy into my life. I love you both with all of my heart.

My deepest gratitude goes to Michele Blood, whose unwavering belief breathes life into my work. She has written this work's foreword and again generously contributed her beautiful chapter, "The Practice of Meditation," which so elegantly weaves these messages into your personal meditation practice. Thank you, Michele, for your steadfast focus on bringing the love of the Divine to people's hearts.

I am so grateful to live in this amazing time! The internet, companies like Amazon and print on demand organisations all allow people to share their gifts with the world. We are truly blessed to be alive now.

Thank you to all those who have taken the time to review this book and offered to share through testimonials. I appreciate every moment of your attention.

I am so grateful for my life. I thank God for every moment and for His loving gift of angels.

"Everyone may open the windows of his Soul and behold the infinite glories of a world far above the universe of sense."

~ Joel S. Goldsmith, author of "The Infinite Way"

Introduction

Welcome to these beautiful pages.

I am so happy to share these messages with you, and I trust that they will ignite a spark in your heart.

Whatever your belief, you can find comfort, inspiration and joy in these words.

MAKE MINE DIVINE is a collection of 31 messages that you can use every month of the year. Select a daily message to inspire you, to use in your meditation and to help take you to that quiet place inside where the real you can be found.

If you wish, you can simply select a number between 1 and 31 to be guided to your message for the day.

My own life has been transformed through discovering the spiritual layer of my existence. I used to be busy, angry and disconnected.

The turning point for me occurred on the day that, in frustration, I called on angels for help. In that moment, I felt an immediate peace and a heart-warming sense of being completely loved.

The idea of communicating with angels may seem foreign to you, as it certainly did to me. It allowed me, though, to connect with this layer of life that I knew existed but seemed so inaccessible to me.

Having an awareness of and a connection with your higher self (the real you) can enrich your physical life in so many wonderful ways. This alignment allows your life to flow more smoothly with fewer struggles and frustrations. A beautiful sense of peace permeates your existence, and the knowledge that all is well allows happiness to flow into your life.

These messages are the words I am inspired to write when I ask angels for guidance to help each of us strengthen this connection. They are filled with wisdom, love and a Light that, when you read them with your heart open, will allow you to *feel* their truth.

I pray that each message blesses you and lights your way to your own beautiful connection with the Divine.

With love,
Hemat Malak

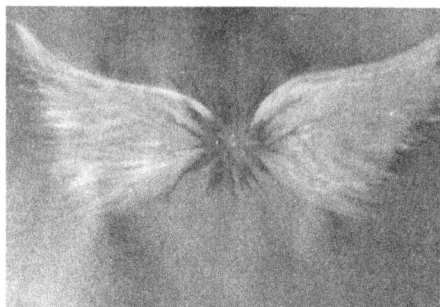

Hello

Allow your divine self
to greet your world.
Meet your children
as the one who is love.
See your family and friends
through eyes bright
with the light of your soul.
Allow the Divine
to walk your world
through your blessed body,
spreading Love and Light
with every step.
Bid farewell to your worries
and relax
as you let God
hello your world.

Add Sweetness

Make delicious your life
with the sweetness of soul.
Liberally sprinkle its grains
of love
over all that is bitter
or sour
or bland.
Sift sweet angel dust
across your creation
so that each morsel
is steeped in love.
Grace the table of the Divine
with your offering –
the toil of your body
sweetened with soul.

Reality

Your senses are finely tuned
to illusion,
convincing you that what you see
and hear
are real.
This world is a reflection
of your mind.
Look to the Source to see reality.
Quiet your good mind
and go within.
Be still
and see with the eyes of your soul;
they look out from your heart.
You will see there is nothing but LOVE,
all-encompassing, breath-taking Love.
Feast your eyes!

Save the Day

Allow your day all its possibilities.
It is filled to the brim
with enough time
to make it beautiful.
Treasure your gifts
as you share them.
Embrace the struggles
as your opportunities to grow.
Love with all of your heart.
Honour everyone on your path
sharing this gift of life with you.
Whatever you are doing
or not doing,
know you are loved completely.
With every fibre of yourself,
both here and beyond,
give thanks for it all.

Child

Dear child of heaven,
you are watched with infinite love
as you learn and grow and live.
Always embraced are you
in the arms of the Divine,
safe,
treasured,
loved beyond measure.
Smooth your brow
with the healing salve
of Light.
Know all is well
and you are growing perfectly
through your lessons.
Relax
and enjoy your days
of wonder.

New Every Moment

Every moment you are new.
Anything you wish to be—
any improvement, any growth,
any wonderfulness you wish to become—
is possible in each moment.
Fill this moment with your wish.
Be what you seek
as you breathe this moment.
You, the earth, your life—
all are new in this moment,
and this precious moment
is all that can fill your hands now.
Shape it, love it, allow it to bloom
before your very eyes.
Care not when it passes.
A new, full, beautiful moment
has arrived again for you.
Precious one, you are so blessed.
Here is your moment
filled with love.

Lean Into Your Life

Your life is illusion.
Do not keep your feet
so firmly planted there
that you lose touch with
your divine source.
Lean into it.
Tread softly.
Learn its priceless lessons
arranged just for you,
all the while knowing
that you are visiting
from afar
and will again one day
stand in eternity.

Comfort

Wait a moment before you reach
for your comfort.
Allow your soul to tell you
how you can be soothed.
Ask to know what you need
to feel better, calmer,
to come back to flow.
In the space you create
you will hear your answer,
and you will not require
the crutches that you curse.
Reach up, child of Light.
Let the heavens carry you
to comfort.

Release Peace

You will feel more peace
when you remove its jailors.
Let go of the needs
you have breathed life into.
The success you imagine is real,
your reflection, which you perfect
to impress the blind,
the pieces of illusion you must possess —
all are shadows
that hold peace at bay.
Allow Divine Light to dissolve them.
Do not fear any loss.
You will feel no pain;
shadows cannot harm you.
Instead, you will breathe again
as the restoring Light of peace
is released into your life.

Your Beauty

Your beauty needs no polish,
no adornment,
no more of this, nor less of that.
Bathed in Light,
you glow
with breathtaking beauty!
The Love that is All
is the fabric of you.
Allow it to fashion you
into a splendid kite,
dancing with glee
in the skies of your world.
Reveal your beauty
as the Divine
flies you to bliss.

Peaceful People

Dear peaceful people,
allow your true nature
to heal your world.
See the good.
In its light,
the shadows will dissolve.
Speak words of love.
Give your others
space for their lessons.
Allow them to learn
as you do.
Call to the Divine in each one,
and that will be
the perfection that emerges.
You do not intend to scorn God.
Respect each of His beloveds.
They are as precious as you.

Awaken Your Heart

Breathe the waking state
into your heart.
Sleep no more
in the busyness of illusion,
tossing and turning
in your dream
of needs and shoulds,
tiring yourself
and wearing yourself down
to nothing.
Stretch through the confines
of your dream state
and open your eyes
to the Light.
Its brilliance will enliven you,
and your heart will swell
with Love.
Live your precious life
awake and full of joy!

Be Driven

Allow yourself to be driven.
Not driven to succeed
or achieve
or any forced impulse
of your making.
Allow yourself to be driven
by the Divine.
Release all the needs
and shoulds
steering you in circles
and empty yourself enough
to be a vehicle
for the Light.
Watch with amazement
and joy
at how skilfully your life is led
by the Driver of creation.
Relax.
Trust.
You are in good hands.

Magnificence

Walk your world
and see the magnificence
around you.
The smallest flower,
the sun's warmth,
the inspired creations of man –
all can be marveled at.
Not least of all,
see yourself.
Look past your reflection
and truly see
the one who walks
this body of yours.
You will catch your breath
at your magnificence!

Promises

As you promise to improve,
to do better,
to please more,
to achieve,
you limit yourself
to the earthly one
who can never be enough.
The hard work of refashioning
your reflection
is not needed.
Your magnificent self,
which can never disappoint,
is all you need be.
Align your body
with your spirit,
beautifully superimposed,
filled to the brim with the Divine,
and walk together
whole and perfect.

Love Your Life

This gift of life you have received
to do with what you will
is the Divine masquerading
as your job, your family, your clothing.
All you see here, in its smallest form,
is the hugeness of Divine Love,
encased in the details of your life.
Cherish every moment, every morsel.
You are in the presence of pure Love,
blessed with the chance to live It.
Love your sacred life,
every joy, every lesson.
You will treasure each moment
when you realise
who is handing it to you.

Magnificent You!

Oh, you are SO loved!
Can you ever know how much?
Every breath you take is precious,
child of the Divine.
Step out of your struggles,
let them go completely.
Pure Love surrounds you;
surrender to its support.
Your tight grasp
is stretching your life
out of shape.
Release your grip
and see it unfold
to its true beauty.
You cannot hide
from your magnificence
any longer!

Discomfort

What is discomforting you?
Be still for a moment and notice
the discomforts that keep you
from happiness.
Let them go.
Yes, you can analyze
and complain
and wallow
and wring from them
every ounce of suffering they hold.
Or you can toss into their waters
a pebble of Truth,
and see them ripple and vanish.
Center yourself in love,
and know all is well.
That is all you need do
at this oasis of life
to see beauty and harmony
and bliss
in the reflections of these waters.

Where God Is

Precious one, if you could know this,
you would catch your breath in bliss
every moment!
So close is God
that your eyelids blink
on the eyes of the Divine.
Dressed as you,
God walks your world,
stepping into your life
through your feet,
peering at creation
through your eyes.
Each soul you pass,
every leaf,
every sound,
every everything,
is the Presence of the Divine.
Feel the fullness in your heart!

Catch the Flow

Your perfect life
with its perfect lessons
and gifts
is flowing right beside you.
Allow yourself to catch the flow.
Release your grasp on everything
that is not working.
The difficulties are your message.
Hear it and let go
so that your hands are empty enough
to be filled with the blessings
waiting for you.
Trust that letting go
will not see you lose anything
of value.
Surrendering to the Divine
opens you to receive
goodness beyond imagination.

Reach

Reach for your light inside.
It is not far
and can be found with just a little searching.
It is bright,
beyond any brilliance you know,
but you must turn to see it.
Open your heart
and invite it out
into your life.
Walk alongside it,
your steps illuminated by it.
Why, you can even converse with it!
All other words you utter
are nonsense
in comparison.
Reach.
It will be the only thing you touch
through the illusion.

After All

After all your sorrows
and after all your joys,
after every feeling and thought,
there is a moment,
empty and available
before your next breath.
Fill it with the awareness
of the Divine.
That tiny moment
will shine its Light
from the spaces between
and flow into your life.
See every empty space
filled with God.
Your heart will sing
as your life is infused
with Love.

Seeing

Let your eyes rest
so that you can see.
The Truth is under the illusion.
Your spiritual eyes
reside in your heart;
use them to view your world.
You will see order instead of chaos,
perfection instead of fault,
and God at the center
of everyone
and everything.
Did you know you were so close to God?
The Divine Presence fills you
and surrounds you.
Close your eyes
and know its bliss!

Be

Be wonderful you.
Relax and let go.
No pretense is needed;
you are perfectly enough
in this very moment.
Don't see perfection everywhere
but in yourself.
You are loved as infinitely
as every other,
and the same Divine
fills you as fills all.
Do justice to the creation
that is you.
No one else can fill your shoes,
wonderful one.
Walk tall and be!

Surrender to the Divine

Dear child of wonder,
trust that you have all you need
to live a blessed life.
Surrender.
Wave the white flag
and step out of your misery.
This is not defeat;
it is victory.
You will conquer struggle
and hopelessness
and fear
when you surrender to the Divine.
Trust.
Allow yourself
to be led away to happiness.

Hunger

When your soul is hungry,
you may find yourself searching
for phantom food
to fill the void.
Filling your body and mind
with sweet nothings
will leave you unsatisfied
and hungry still.
No food of this world,
no distraction of mind
can nourish your soul.
Allow the Light to fill
your emptiness
and see the yearning leave you.
Indulge your soul
in the bliss of love, and
at God's banquet,
you will sit,
restored and content.

Stop and Drink

Sip the water of the earth
and become one with her.
Align yourself with her
so that your body is whole
and healthy
and ready for the Divine.
As you drink,
become one with the oceans.
As the waves embrace you,
feel the waves of love
in your heart.
Allow life to connect you
and awaken your senses
to the Divine.

You

You are all there is.
All of nature,
all humanity,
all emotion,
all knowledge,
all creations of man
and God.
You are this All.
The you of this earth
and the you of eternity
encompass everything.
The Divine fills you
and IS you.
Oh, the bliss
of housing God!

Fill Yourself with Light

Allow the Light of the Heavens to fill you —
not just your body, all of you —
so that it illuminates everything around you
as you walk through life.
Shadows will vanish as you pass,
and the Light will heal and bless
and bring whatever is needed
to your brothers and sisters.
Your world can change in an instant
when the Divine can shine on it.
Feel it now in your heart,
its warmth and love infusing every cell
and more,
as it shines you to your true glory.

The Love of God

The Love of God is nearer
than you imagine.
The air caressing your face,
the blood coursing through your veins,
the breaths you draw –
you are surrounded
and filled
with God's infinite Love.
Be still and feel its bliss.
This warmth in your heart
is all you need
to sustain you.
How divine to be loved so!
Precious child,
there is nothing you can fear.
Walk this world,
joyful
and enveloped in Love.

Trust

Trust that all is well.
You are never alone
and never far from Love.
Child of perfection,
allow yourself this comfort.
Know you are precious
to the Divine
and your life is unfolding
perfectly.
Relax into your life
and trust each day
as it dawns for you.
Step out just enough
to trust God with your life.
Release all that you grip
and trust that it falls
into God's palm.

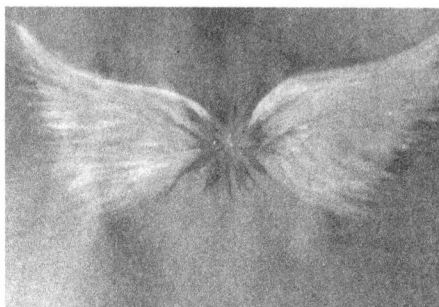

The Practice of Meditation

by Michele Blood

Hello again, beautiful reader. My dear friend, Hemat Malak, asked me to write a section for her readers who wish to go a little deeper into their spiritual practice. We are going to speak about *the practice of meditation!* Life can become more beautiful than any human dream. This chapter is not long in page number, but may it assist you in bringing more joy, power and peace into your heart and life.

Meditation with spiritual contemplation is beautiful, powerful and beyond words. It connects us to love, and love is the most creative and powerful thing in the world. Love is a *real* power and, it is pure, beautiful and can help you create a life of fulfilment and *real magic*. The practice of meditation connects us to this love and helps us connect to our soul/higher-self faster than any other method known. Of course, this is not only *our* opinion; this has been taught by every great master throughout history. However, *thinking* about meditating and *actually practicing* meditation are two very different things.

These instructions will help assist you if...

First, you have *never* meditated before or...

Second, if you *do* meditate but would like to bring the heat up in your practice and really feel its awesome power.

Meditation is a practice of making the mind still and connecting with our God-Self. Stillness is the mind's natural state. It is only when we become frustrated with the things that we desire or the things that we fear that we lose our natural state of peace and go down into lower states of mind. When our mind is engaged in meditation and mindfulness throughout the day, lower states of mind eventually lose their power over us.

So, how do we stay mindful?

Well, we...

- Contemplate beautiful truths, such as those that are in this beautiful book by Hemat
- Strive to be happy
- Feel grateful for every moment
- Be calm
- Do not judge
- Stay unattached to the *how*
- Bring power and focus into every action

We are not practicing meditation to become passive beings, no, no, no! We are practicing meditation and mindfulness because it makes us *much* stronger, resilient and confident individuals.

The combination of meditation with powerful focused action will allow our life projects to be realized and completed with great fulfilment and...SUCCESS! Our minds will no longer be focused on what we *do not want*, but instead will be focused with love on the task at hand, in the moment and with joy. When we work on a project with joy, magical powers of Light come in to assist. This Holy Light, which is the source of all creation, blesses everyone. People will be more attracted to your work than *ever* before.

It is important to have *big goals* and *beautiful intentions* for our life. When we are drawn to "The Good Life," which is our Divine birth right, this is our Divine self saying, *"YES, you deserve this. Go for it."* God's duty is also our own duty; it is one and the same. However, if we have trouble focusing, things may never get completed to our satisfaction and then, we will have no fulfilment. We may eventually turn away from thoughts of "The Good Life" and have our goals turn into powerless *wishful thinking* experiences of frustration.

What if I am agnostic? Can meditation help me?

Even if you are agnostic, look at meditation as physicians do. It has been well documented that people who meditate regularly have lower blood pressure and, generally, are healthier, happier human beings. So, do it even if the word 'God' is not your thing. Put a smile on your face and be still. Before you sit down to meditate, do whatever you can to put yourself into a happy mindset.

Meditation will also make you more sensitive to your surroundings, and you will begin to desire to release some of *the stuff* from your environment, career and personal life. You will want more order and refinement. This is a *good* thing. An uncluttered life will awaken within you a very pure and simple view of Infinite Mind. A cluttered life will just keep you, well,... cluttered.

What we see and experience on the outside powerfully affects everything else in our lives. With disorder, we will just never get to what matters the most, *peace*, *freedom* and *Light*. We take our clutter with us everywhere we go. Going to a spa for the day will not release the clutter; even if it is taken from our vision, it will still be with us. Simply leaving doesn't change anything. We have to simplify our lives *and* our minds. We must focus on the inner self and less on our outer self. We need to spend time quietly working and letting our mind go beyond our work into The Infinite. This is true mindfulness.

Creating Your Own Space

Designate a special place/space where you live to meditate in your home. Clean this area *really* well, as this will release old energies. When we meditate, it is best to have clean energy. Buy a brand new mat on which to sit. Light a beautiful candle and some incense if you feel this will give a calming vibration to your mind. Create a little altar made of natural material, such as wood. All items, including your mat, *must* be brand new and, **most importantly,** everything in this space must only have been purchased by you and *be brand new,* as you do not wish to draw other energies and lines of attention into the meditation space. Fresh flowers or living green plants are also good.

If you do not live alone, ask your roommate or partner to please respect *your* special place. Do not allow anyone else to meditate on your mat. When meditating, more power and Light is brought into this space so that each time you meditate in *your space,* it will become easier, as you are using the Light that has already been created to flow through and expand.

Do not meditate in bed if you find it difficult to sleep afterwards, as meditation increases energy. Meditation is not meant to make you sleepy; it is a very focused practice that later gives you much energy and life-force. You will be increasing *life*!

Creating Intention through Contemplative Meditation

Contemplative meditation practice can eventually lead us to a moment of pure silence, where, at last, all thoughts have stopped. This exquisite silence is deeper than any ocean. This is when power, light and guidance come to us directly from Source. When this happens, it is no longer our own thoughts coming through us. We have become an instrument of God's own mind. Eternity speaks to us. This is truly the mystical way. Mysticism is simply God speaking to us, but, for this to happen, we must learn to be still and stop our thoughts.

Now, let's go into some instructions on how to proceed with this contemplative practice.

Intention

1) Select any page of Hemat's beautiful book and read the angel message. Read it again out loud slowly. Then...

2) Breathe in through your nose deeply, hold it and then exhale slowly through your mouth. Do this three times.

3) Now, we no longer focus on the words of the message; we just ask the Divine to allow you to be open to the truth of the message in your life. Then, we let go…

4) Now, continue into the silence until you feel peaceful and an *all is well* feeling. Continue now in the silence and allow God to speak *through you* as a feeling or small, still voice. Now let go…surrender…

At the end of your meditation, take a bow of gratitude and say, "Thank you, my soul, today is already a magical day."

This way, our day is governed and directed by our Divine Presence, not our human mind, which can be a trickster and sometimes will simply *not shut up!* So, begin with an intention to connect with God and contemplate the message you have read. Then, go into the silence for approximately 10-15 minutes. In total, this would take approximately 15 minutes. Of course, sit and meditate for longer if you can at this stage without your mind wandering too much. Remember, we cannot think of two things at the same time.

Music and Meditation

This world presently has over seven billion souls living on it, and this number is rising rapidly. So, of course, in this day and age it is *much* harder than it was in a time such as the ancient Egyptian era to meditate. Why? Because we have all of these other people's thoughts and lines of attention continually bombarding our sensitive psychic minds. This is where music can help and where the very cool, modern iPods come in handy. We have added a recommended listing of meditation music CDs from various artists at the end of this segment.

So, what you do is…

1) Sit down on your meditation mat and *smile* before you begin, as this will help open your heart chakra. The intention is to bring in peace and joy. Now, feel gratitude. It must be sincere. We all must have someone or something we are grateful for or to. Bringing in this feeling of gratitude is vital, as this is love.

2) Now, breathe in through your nose deeply, hold it and then exhale slowly through your mouth. Do this three to five times, as this will help your mind to quiet down. Now, put on the music you have selected and listen. Let the waves of beautiful sounds fill your being. If your mind wanders, just keep going back to the music and be still.

3) After a few minutes, or one track, focus on your heart chakra and think of a word, like *oneness, harmony, bliss, peace* or *joy.* So, whenever the mind wanders, go back to the music for a few minutes, and then, back to your heart. Do this for fifteen minutes or longer until you feel still and peaceful, then simply let go.

4) After you have listened to two to four tracks of music and have felt at one with the music and at one with your heart, you will have achieved that feeling of peace, joy and unity with the Universe. Next, bow, give thanks, get up and go about your day.

All beings are made of electrical currents, and our bodies are outlets of this energy. The chakras are like an electrical outlet strip, loosely aligned with our spine, which we can plug into. As electricity comes from the ether of the cosmos, once we awaken the Light within us by plugging into Eternity, we are then true extensions of the universe.

Please feel no impatience with yourself or frustration if your mind will not shut up, as after some practice this *does* work. It is still benefiting you, and, even if you do not feel it, *you are getting results.* If you follow this simple method, eventually, you will find that outside intruding thoughts will cease, and you will be able to sit quietly in a peaceful state with or without music. Have patience and be consistent. Remember that anything new takes practice. You would not expect to be able to play Mozart after your first piano lesson.

At first, do not attempt to do this for more than ten to fifteen minutes, unless you feel like it. You are doing this only for a conscious realization of your unity with Spirit or to make contact with God. We are not attempting to see "light" or to have "experiences." If they do come, great! But, if we become too fascinated with these "experiences," we could lose sight of the main focus, which is to be in the silence, by making way too much of them. Keep it simple, (KISS: Keep it Simple and Spiritual) and smile!

Each time you practice meditation, even if for only three minutes, you are adding more light and power of intention to your focus and more light to our world. It affects everything.

Before we go onto to the next suggested meditation, here are some suggested music CDs that hold beautiful music that will help *sweep* you into your infinite, beautiful inner self. Set your intentions high, and may God pour blessings of great increases of abundance and life to you today and always. Remember to smile and breathe.

Meditation Music Suggestions – Anything that you feel is beautiful, opens up your heart, you can feel at one with and does not have too much singing, unless it is choirs (Mozart, etc.)

Let's Get Metaphysical: www.EMusiVation.com

Lake Melva Meditation: www.YellowBell.com

Diane Arkenstone: Jewel in the Sun (iTunes)

Tangerine Dream: Seven Years in Tibet (iTunes)

David Arkenstone: Altantis (iTunes)

Mozart: (iTunes)

Mysteria: Chasing the Divine (iTunes)

Visualization Practice

Now, this is *not* a guided meditation, nor is it visualization. This is a different form of meditation, as now, we are going into our meditation not to get anything per say, but to only connect with the Divine Presence. This suggested practice is to help those who find it easier to visualize to experience the Divine Presence. We think using meditation music along with this suggestion may also help tremendously to get *in tune* with the peace, love and joy that *is* the Divine Presence.

1) Sit down on your meditation mat and quiet down your mind. Breathe in through your nose, doing your best to breathe in deeply through *both nostrils,* hold it and then release slowly by exhaling through your mouth. Do this three or four times. Think the

thought of *peace, peace* with each intake of breath and with each exhale.

2) Now, imagine a vast ocean. This ocean has thousands of soft, beautiful waves that go on forever. Feel that you are one with this beautiful ocean. Visualize and *feel* that each wave in the ocean is softly moving over you and caressing you with Love and Light. Each wave is peace; each wave is joy and love. With each wave, you are feeling an increase of more and more joy.

3) Now, feel yourself sinking slowly into the ocean's depths where all is calm, peaceful and serene. After doing this for a while, allow feelings of joy, peace and love to enter *your heart.*

4) Now, as you go down deeper into the ocean's depths, imagine the waves have gone down with you and have transformed into soft, luminous, golden rings. See these beautiful soft, luminous, golden rings come down from above and softly encircle your whole body, one after another after another. These are waves of Light, and you are one with them. See these golden rings softy dissolve into your body and then fill your whole space with soft, golden, luminous Light. Such exquisite peace is now part of you, *as you.* After a while, let your mind go. Stop visualizing and just focus on your heart chakra and breathe. Continue this for as long as you wish.

Your mind will return to this world when the peace and light have been absorbed.

Also, gazing at an object for the first half of your meditation practice helps tremendously. Choose a flower, a candle or a picture of your favourite deity and gently gaze at this object. Blink if you need to, but after 10 minutes or so, close your eyes and just *feel love* in your heart space.

The suggestions you have just read are to help you focus and become one with your spirit, your very own beautiful soul, which is your *guardian angel* of Light. So now, you may see what *real prayer* is. *Real prayer* is what we experience *after* we have set our intention, spoken our words and let go. The silence is where the *real magic* happens and what real prayer is.

May these suggestions help you bring in more Light, power and prosperity consciousness. It is our intention that each person who reads these words and practices is blessed and experiences an increase of all that is good in the world, especially the *real world* of Light.

If you are having a challenge with your meditation practice, do not give up. Allow these loving and all wise words by the great soul, Paramahansa Yogananda assist you...

"Your trouble with meditation is that you don't persevere long enough to get results. That is why you never know the power of a focused mind. If you let muddy water stand still for a long time, the mud will settle at the bottom, and the water will become clear. In meditation, when the mud of your restless thoughts begins to settle, the power of God begins to reflect in the clear waters of your consciousness."

Hemat and I wish you an increase of life, an increase of all good. Now, everyone, thank your soul by practicing the stillness and beauty of meditation and contemplating these beautiful, Divine messages. Things will change in your favour. Any fire can be rekindled in your career, in your personal relationships and in any area of your life!

This time, the excitement will be with more enthusiasm and passion than you ever experienced before. This is where the magic that is within you comes out to play. Rekindle that fire. Do not ever again take life for granted. Say to your inner magical self, *"No matter what is happening, I am going to trust this magic that is within me. I am going to believe in this magic and love."* Whatever you do, do it with enthusiasm and gratitude. Open your heart as you read Hemat's beautiful, Divine angel messages, and go out now and *live, sing it out! I am truly grateful for my life!*

May your life be filled with peace and joy, and may the Holy Light fill your consciousness with bliss.

In Love and Oneness,
Michele and Hemat

(Michele Blood's websites are www.MysticalSuccessClub.com and www.Musivation.com)

About the Author

Hemat Malak, award-winning author, loved writing poetry as a child.

It was not until she experienced the frustrations of an adult life gone wrong and the blessings that came to turn everything around that she wrote again.

After a failed marriage, she found herself alone with two young children (the youngest with additional needs), feeling angry and disillusioned. Her search for answers led to a beautiful connection with angels that lit her spirit with the love of the Divine.

"Malak" means *angel* in Arabic and *messenger* in Hebrew, a lovely synchronicity. From her home in Sydney, Australia, Hemat writes to ignite in others their own connection to the Divine.

She continues to share angel messages on her website, AngelHeartLight, at http://angelheartlight.com.

Other Books by This Author

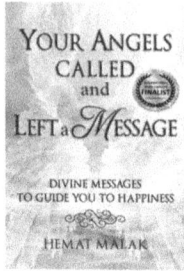

Your Angels Called and Left a Message

EBook available at angelheartlight.com, Amazon and most eBook retailers.

Print Book available at Amazon and many print book retailers.

120 beautiful messages to nourish your soul.

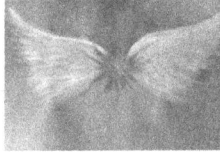

If you enjoyed this book, you can share your experience and assist other readers by leaving a review at your favourite retailer.

The author's page on Amazon can be found by searching for *Hemat Malak* on Amazon.com.

You are welcome to visit AngelHeartLight on Facebook and Google+ for more inspiration.